OPEN DOORS

EMBRACING YOUR SEASON OF OPEN DOORS

ANTHONIA ADEYEYE

OPEN DOORS

EMBRACING YOUR SEASON OF OPEN DOORS

ANTHONIA ADEYEYE

OPEN DOORS
Embracing Your Season of Open Doors
Copyright © 2016 by **Anthonia Adeyeye**

ISBN: 978-1-944652-06-7

Printed in the United States of America. All rights reserved solely by the publisher. This book or parts thereof may not be reproduced in any form, stored in a retrieval system, or transmitted in any form by any means - electronic, mechanical, photocopy. Unless otherwise noted, Bible quotations are taken from the Holy Bible, New King James Version. Copyright 1982 by Thomas Nelson, Inc., publishers. Used by permission.

Published By:
Cornerstone Publishing
Info@thecornerstonepublishers.com
www.thecornerstonepublishers.com
516.547.4999

Ordering Information:

To order books and CDs by Dr. Anthonia Adeyeye, please write to:

Dr. Anthonia Adeyeye
Adeyeye Evangelistic Ministries (AEM)
P.O Box 810
West Hempstead, NY 11552
E-mail: dranthonia@alcministries.com

Website: www.alccwinnershouse.org

CONTENTS

Dedication..7

Acknowledgement......................................9

Introduction...11

Chapter 1

Supernatural Encounters............................15

Chapter 2

Doorways To Destiny.................................21

Chapter 3

Understanding Open Doors........................27

Chapter 4

Knowing The God Of The Open Doors.........35

Chapter 5

The True God..47

Chapter 6

The God That Opens And Closes....................57

Chapter 7

Infinite Possibilities..63

Chapter 8

God Makes No Mistakes.................................77

Chapter 9

Keeping Your Cool In Hot Situations.............91

Chapter 10

Adversaries Of Your Doors............................101

Chapter 11

Power To Maximize Your Doors...................113

THE GREATEST PRAYER......................133

DEDICATION

This book is lovingly dedicated to my heavenly Father.

Lord, you have asked me many times, "Daughter, where are my books?"

The first of all good things belongs to you; so here it is Dad, the first of your books. Thank you for loving me unconditionally, thank you for saving me, thank you for not leaving me in my filthiness and chasing of the wind.

I love you Dad, and I am YOURS FOREVER.

ACKNOWLEDGEMENTS

My love and deep appreciation go to the love of my life, Dr. Festus Adeyeye. Truly, you are more than the 'cream cheese on my bagel', 'the syrup on my pumpkin pancake', 'the cow-foot in my okra soup', 'the flying fish and the ox-tail', and 'the only bright light in a dark room'. You are the best thing that has happened to me after Christ. I love you.

To my 'ten children', thank you for the shirt you gave me, with the inscription, 'Mother of Ten'. Thank you for making mothering so pleasurable and fruitful. May your hearts be ever tender and sensitive to God's loving touch. I pray that you will yield yourselves daily to this Awesome God. I love you all, piece by piece.

To my biological brothers and sisters all over the world, especially to my younger sisters - Niyi and Jumoke – I love you two so much.

To my Abundant Life Christian Ministries family

all over the world, thank you for believing in God and in us. The God of breakthrough who has called us will forever shine His light in your lives. Your godly heart desires shall be granted and you will laugh last in every area of your lives.

To all ALCC Pastors, Elders, Ministers, and Workers - you are the greatest bunch on earth! Your godly dreams will be fulfilled in Jesus name.

To all God lovers all over the world, may your love for God be infectious, may the kingdom of our Father enlarge in the billions in Jesus name.

To my father, who is 'home with the Lord', thank you for instilling confidence in me. To my mom - Mama Olayemi - I know that God will give you a special crown for raising all of us so well.

And to my three sisters who are home with the Lord - what a great fun time we had together on earth. I love you all!

INTRODUCTION

Dear reader, I congratulate you for picking up this book. I believe it will completely change your life and place you on the pathway of perpetual success. Beyond that, it will actually transform your perception of success and failure.

There are two kinds of doors - physical and spiritual. Physical doors are doors that can be seen with the physical or natural eyes. Spiritual doors, on the other hand, cannot be seen with the natural eyes but they are very much in existence. Also, while physical doors are limited to 'a means of entry and exit', spiritual doors go beyond this. Put simply, while physical doors are mere accesses to places, positions and endeavors, spiritual doors are all these plus the fact that they provide ACCESS to ASSETS.

I have encountered many Christians who were frustrated because their hard work seemed not to be generating commensurate successful results. A lady once spoke to me about being employed for twenty-two years without being promoted. The reason for this was not clear to her, but the reason was simple; while the lady had physically gained entrance into the job through employment, she had not gained entrance through the spiritual door. While she seemed to have gotten the job through the physical door, she had actually been 'kept out' of it because the spiritual door to the job had been shut against her.

It was for the purpose of unveiling such Kingdom secrets that this book was written. It is a book of IMPARTATION. As you read through it and pray, anointing for accelerated progress will come upon you to make you unstoppable on your path to success. As you imbibe and apply the revelations therein, things you have attempted and failed at, and even things you have not been able to attempt at all, will be accomplished suddenly and successfully.

I had a similar experience in the writing of this book. Before now, I had made several attempts to write my first book but all had met with brick wall upon brick wall. I had many uncompleted manuscripts and uncountable Holy Ghost-inspired prayer nuggets, but no book came out of them. I would start writing a manuscript with excitement and then the brick wall would emerge, and all the excitement would go down the drain. God eventually used Dr. Festus Adeyeye (my spiritual father, covering, mentor, and who happens to be my husband) and Dr. Mike Murdock (a truly anointed man of God) to destroy the brick walls and open the spiritual door that transformed me to an author!

And you won't believe this. What I had not been able to do for years – to write a book - was done in one week. Yes, ONE WEEK! What's more, God said that the same "open door anointing" that came on me while writing this book will come upon every reader. From this moment, access is granted to you to achieve whatever good thing you have always wanted to do in Jesus name. Grace is also released to do with ease whatever you want to do in righteousness.

CHAPTER 1

SUPERNATURAL ENCOUNTERS

I wish to share with you some supernatural experiences that confirm the existence of spiritual doors. But first, you must know that there are three realms of existence: the natural world, the spirit world, and the underworld.

In the natural world, which is this earth, there are things that you can see with the physical eyes and there are things you cannot see with the physical eyes. There are germs, bacteria and other organisms that can only be seen using special instruments such as the microscope. Although these microscopic organisms exist, the physical eyes cannot see them. Similarly, there are places that the physical eyes cannot see. Now, just because the physical eyes cannot see these places does not mean that they are not in existence.

SPIRIT REALM

One place the physical or natural eyes cannot see is the SPIRIT REALM. I assume, reader, that you must have lived in more than two locations since you were born. If so, can you envision or mentally view the house or street of your birth? Do you remember some of your neighbors and friends? What about your first school and some other places you visited? I'm sure your answers to these questions will be in the affirmative.

The point is, you can see the place of your birth with your inner eyes, even though you are no longer physically in the area. That you are no longer in the place of your birth does not automatically cancel its existence. This is the same with the spirit world. Just because you cannot see it with your physical eyes does not nullify its existence. Also, as there are people currently residing in the neighborhood of your youth – whom you cannot see for now - so also are there spirits residing in the spirit realm.

Let me re-emphasize that even though you and I cannot see the spirit realm, it does exist, and it is as real as the world we both live in. By God's special grace, I have been privileged to visit the spirit realm many times. For a long time, I had been reluctant to share these supernatural experiences. I wanted to see if there were people in the Bible that had similar experiences. The Holy Spirit then showed me that such people were indeed many. Such people include Prophet Ezekiel, Paul the Apostle and John the Beloved.

STRIKING RECOLLECTIONS

On Tuesday, 27th July 2004, I had a memorable 'out-of-body' experience. Actually, I've had a number of such experiences in which my spirit would leave my body to do whatever I was instructed to do. On one occasion, I travelled through a pathway lit up by a very bright light. I found myself in a dark hospital room, filled with Muslims. The hospital was in another country in a different location from where I resided. I was instructed to preach to these Muslims, bedridden with different ailments. As I did,

I showed them the path of light that I travelled in to reach the dark room where they were. I told them if they would receive the Light, they would never be in darkness again. They all received the Lord, and got healed immediately (To God be the glory!).

Back to my 27th July experience. I had just had a time of worship and prayer with the Lord, after which I laid down to sleep. Shortly after, my spirit came out of my body. I looked down to see that what I called my body was still there on the bed, like a shell. It was like the 'apartment' that the 'real me' - my spirit was living in. I enjoyed the boundless freedom so much that I said, "This is the way life should be in the physical realm".

Just then, I saw a door that opened to another level, higher than the flight zone, where I was. At the door was someone like an angel, looking so resplendent. Behind the angel were bright and beautiful lights. The angel beckoned on me to come through the door into the higher realm. In my spirit, I knew I was being given an opportunity to visit heaven. So, I asked myself, "Am I dead?" and I heard my spirit say to the angel, "No, I am not ready to die yet". As soon as I said this, my spirit came back into my body. My spirit 'wore' my lifeless body on the bed, step-by-step, as one would wear a piece of clothing.

SALIENT REFLECTION

I would have loved to inform you that I actually visited heaven during that particular experience, but I didn't. I believe the reason I responded the way I did during the encounter was that I allowed my mind to interfere with what God wanted to show me. In other words, I demonstrated a lack of faith in God.

Later on in this book, I will emphasize the importance of believing and trusting God wholeheartedly. This is the only way to please God and obtain blessings from Him. In fact, the new definition of faith that the Holy Spirit gave me as I wrote the pages of this book was, "Faith is following God blindly".

Just assume that your physical eyes are not there and that God is your guide. If you cannot see physically, you would trust and obey your guide completely. God is our Guide, and He has given us His Holy Spirit to guide and help us throughout the journey of life. For you to safely arrive at your appointed destination, you must learn to follow the

Holy Spirit 'blindly'.

I pray for you, reader, that God will give you insight into the deep things in His heart for you and for the world around you. I pray that the hunger for God will consume you more than the hunger for anyone or anything else. I pray that God takes you on a deeper walk with Him. I pray that your spirit, soul, and body be sanctified through and through in Jesus name. (Amen).

CHAPTER 2

DOORWAYS TO DESTINY

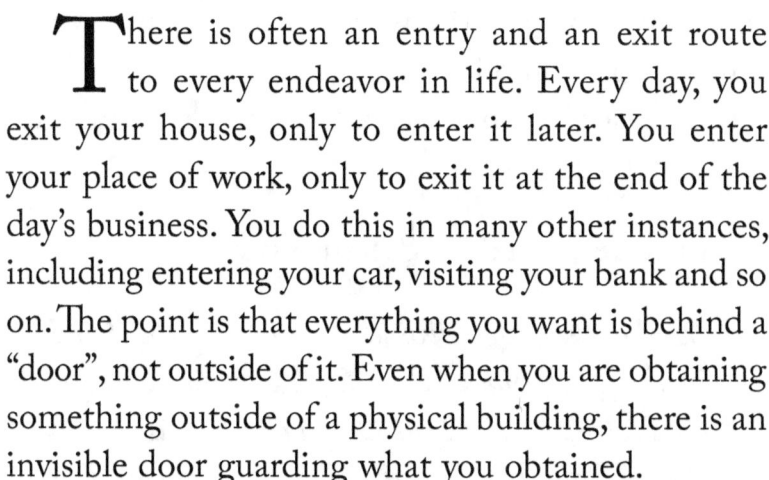

There is often an entry and an exit route to every endeavor in life. Every day, you exit your house, only to enter it later. You enter your place of work, only to exit it at the end of the day's business. You do this in many other instances, including entering your car, visiting your bank and so on. The point is that everything you want is behind a "door", not outside of it. Even when you are obtaining something outside of a physical building, there is an invisible door guarding what you obtained.

There is a door that enters the world. Through

this, many activities are conducted such as angels ascending and descending, children being born and people dying, and so many other spiritual transactions. As a reader of this book, I congratulate you because it means you have not exited into the heavens and you can still enter and exit into the different doors for earthly business transactions.

DOMINANCE OF SPIRITUAL DOORS

As I mentioned in the introduction, there are spiritual doors that cannot be seen with the physical eyes. The 'brick wall' that caused me to fail severally in my attempts at writing a book was actually a spiritual door into the world of successful authors. The lack of promotion that the dear lady experienced in her place of work was a spiritual door into that company.

In Revelation 3: 7- 8, Jesus says:

"And to the angel (divine messenger) of the church in Philadelphia write: "These are the words of the Holy One, the True One, He who has the key [to the house] of David, He who opens and no one will [be able to] shut, and He who shuts and

no one opens: 'I know your deeds. See, I have set before you an open door which no one is able to shut, for you have a little power, and have kept My word, and have not renounced or denied My name." (AMP)

Christ's message here is both illustrative and instructive. More importantly, it underscores the supremacy of spiritual doors over physical doors. Members of the church in Philadelphia (a city in the then Asia Minor - now known as Turkey) had been experiencing aggravations from those who were bragging that they were the true Jewish people. These people were claiming authenticity of faith and superiority of position over the Philadelphian church. Jesus saw the frustrations of this church and how their detractors had been making it difficult for them to fulfill their purpose. He therefore assured them that it would no longer matter what their oppressors were doing to frustrate them. He said, "I have set before you an open door...that door will cause your enemies to bow for you, and they will acknowledge that you are the apple of my eyes."

This is one of the things that a spiritual door does - it causes notable and enviable breakthroughs. Those who claimed to be the real Jews over the Philadelphian church might still continue to brag, but the spiritual door opened by Christ would cause such success and glory that would surprise and subdue the 'fake Jews'.

It is worth repeating that physical doors are doors that people can see with the natural eyes, hold with the natural hands, and can be opened or closed by people. Spiritual doors are in the realm that cannot be seen with the physical eyes. Basically then, Jesus is saying through the above scripture that people may close physical doors against you, but He has opened spiritual doors for you. If your spiritual door is open, you can successfully transact businesses in the physical realm and become who God has ordained you to be. People may close physical doors against you, but Jesus has opened your spiritual doors!

DISTINCTIVE DEDUCTIONS

My General Overseer, Dr. Adeyeye once made a remarkable statement. He said, "Just because a person has physically entered a location (a country, business center, profession or any place at all), does not mean the spiritual door of the place is opened for the person". And when your spiritual door is not open, you may be at a spot for twenty-two years like the lady I earlier mentioned, or be fruitlessly attempting to achieve a goal for many years like me.

Physical entry into a location or business does not mean spiritual entry into the location or business. And if there is no spiritual entry, there can be no physical success. On the contrary, a person who has successfully gained entrance through both the physical and the spiritual doors of a location or a business will experience tremendous success.

One main reason people go through hardship, failure and stagnancy in life generally is because a certain spiritual door has been closed on them. Essentially then, three simple formulas can be deduced from the foregoing:

- Closed physical door and closed spiritual door = hardship and failure.

- Open physical door and open spiritual door = Outstanding success.

- Closed physical door but open spiritual door (through divine intervention) = Guaranteed success.

CHAPTER 3

UNDERSTANDING OPEN DOORS

So far, I have made many references to open doors and the corresponding results. But what exactly are open doors?

Let's look at Revelation 3: 7-8 again:

"And to the angel (divine messenger) of the church in Philadelphia write: "These are the words of the Holy One, the True One, He who has the key [to the house] of David, He who opens and no one will [be able to] shut, and He who shuts and no one opens: 'I know your deeds. See, I have set

before you an open door which no one is able to shut, for you have a little power, and have kept My word, and have not renounced or denied My name."

The 'open door' referred to by Jesus is an access to assets, which automatically positions the beneficiary beyond ordinary living. A person enjoying open door begins to enjoy extraordinary results in the same areas where he or she had suffered pain, hurts, and frustrations. What causes this extraordinary transformation is the torrent of assets that is released through the open doors.

The Web dictionary has the following definitions of asset(s):

- A useful and desirable thing or quality - such as organizational ability.
- A single item of ownership having exchange value.
- Items of ownership convertible into cash.
- Total resources of a person or business (Such as: cash, notes, securities, inventories, goodwill, fixtures, machinery, or real estate).
- All property available for the payment of

debts.

My definition of asset as inspired by the Holy Spirit is: "anything or anyone (both in the realm you can see and that which you cannot see], given to you by God to solve your problems."

This is the reason that when God opens a door for you, you suddenly begin to achieve success where you had failed. Burdens are lifted, mountains are removed, yokes are broken and protracted dilemmas are easily resolved due to the open door.

MY EXPERIENCE

Let me provide further details on how the challenge of writing my first book was conquered. I mentioned in the preface that, for many years, writing a book was an uphill task for me. The Holy Spirit would nudge me year after year, saying: "Where are my books? You owe me books".

Tired of trying and failing, I urged family members and friends to pray for me and even challenge me by asking about the books. My children would ask, "Mummy, when will the book be ready?"

Actually, it is not that it is compulsory to write books. But God specifically told me He had deposited treasures in me that must change billions of people. Yet year after year, I had no success in this area. I had different unfinished manuscripts all over, notes that could be generated into four or five books; but I just couldn't put things together. Until Dr. Festus gave a sermon on 'Open Door', and another one on 'Divine Acceleration'. Those sermons simply lit up my path. Interestingly, I had given sermons on the same topics, but somehow I never prayed that God should open the door for me to write books.

Not long after, Dr. Mike Murdock came to New York. During his sermon, he declared that there were people in the meeting who would do in few days what they had not been able to achieve in years. Right there, I asked God to release upon my life the grace of authorship upon Dr. Murdock. I received the prophetic release and sowed a seed of faith to complete the spiritual transaction.

I knew by the impression of the Holy Spirit that I had received grace that night to become a successful author. This is because immediately after that ministration, the Holy Spirit instructed me to write the book you are reading. I was able to write the first three chapters in just FOUR HOURS! I was so surprised at the ease with which I wrote. I just kept thanking God.

The Holy Spirit joked with me, saying, "Daughter, what were you expecting? Would I allow you to struggle and toil when you specifically asked me to open this door? Would I allow you to write a book on open doors and not truly open doors for you?"

EXTENDED IMPARTATION

As I said before, the Holy Spirit informed me that this first book is not an ordinary book; it is a book of impartation that will release anointing upon every reader and help them to achieve supernatural results, just like He helped me with the writing of the book. What an awesome God we serve! To Him be all the glory.

As you read this book, therefore, anointing for open doors is being released upon you. Assets are being showered upon you in the areas you need open doors in Jesus name. Don't forget that asset is anything (wisdom, favor, peace, joy, promotion, or any other thing you need) or anyone (People in high places, low places, angels, even your enemies) given by God to give you extraordinary results.

Based upon the different definitions, assets can be:

- Wisdom
- Favor
- Utterance or eloquence
- Anointing
- Entrance or access
- Connection to people you need
- Money
- Ideas
- Excellent spirit (especially for students, business people, and professionals)
- Innovations
- Inspirations
- Skillfulness
- Competence

Truly the list is endless. This is the reason you must call upon God to open doors for you. Your life will be radically transformed, with visible, meaningful and numerous successful results.

Doors are opening for you right now in Jesus name. Every satanic hold is broken, evil expectation is shattered, and every negative proclamation against you is captured and destroyed permanently in Jesus name. You will begin to see notable and numerous successes in the areas of your heart desires in Jesus name.

CHAPTER 4

KNOWING THE GOD OF THE OPEN DOORS

In order to build your faith and position you to receive the manifold blessings that God wants to release upon you, you need to understand the meanings behind the different titles that Jesus used to introduce Himself to the Philadelphian Church.

Generally in His messages to the seven churches in the book of Revelation, Jesus introduced Himself in different ways to each church. Let me take you through some of them:

"To the angel (divine messenger) of the church in

Ephesus write:"These are the words of the One who holds [firmly] the seven stars [which are the angels or messengers of the seven churches] in His right hand, the One who walks among the seven golden lampstands (the seven churches)" (2:1)

"And to the angel (divine messenger) of the church in Smyrna write:"These are the words of the First and the Last [absolute Deity, the Son of God] who died and came to life [again]" (2:8).

"And to the angel (divine messenger) of the church in Pergamum write: "These are the words of Him who has and wields the sharp two-edged sword [in judgment.]" (2:12)

"To the angel (divine messenger) of the church in Sardis write: "These are the words of Him who has the seven Spirits of God and the seven stars..." (3:1)

"And to the angel (divine messenger) of the church in Philadelphia write: "These are the words of the Holy One, the True One, He who has the key [to the house] of David, He who opens and no one will [be able to] shut, and He who shuts and no one opens" (3:7)

WHAT'S IN A TITLE?

There were cogent reasons for which Jesus introduced Himself with different titles to the different churches. One, He did so based on the state of each church - their deeds, challenges and general conditions. Two, he wanted the churches to pay attention to the significance of each title He used for Himself. The aim was to build up their faith, as well as to effect meaningful and positive changes, where necessary.

Christ's approach to the churches equally applies to us today. Just as He introduced Himself differently to the churches, so also does He know you personally and cares for you individually. Families and friends might have disappointed you, but Jesus is here to let you know that He loves you unconditionally.

So, what exactly does Jesus want you to know about the glorious titles He used for Himself? What are the implications of these different names? Let's take His introduction to the church of Philadelphia as a case study. He says in Revelation 3:7:

"...*These are the WORDS of the Holy One...*"

There is a clear distinction between words from people to people, and Words from God to people. People can play with words and say what they don't mean, but God does not joke with His words. Jesus wanted the Philadelphian church (and the present church) to know that His words are not mere words; they are SPIRITS and LIFE (John 6:63).

SIGNIFICANCE OF CHRIST'S WORDS

1. Christ's words are spirits. When God's angels (who are also spirits) are on assignments, they don't go back to God without completing their assigned responsibilities. They don't go back to report that assignments are too difficult. Every assignment must be completed, no matter the opposition (Daniel 10:12-21).

In the same way, the word that has gone out of God's mouth concerning your life will not return to Him without fulfilling its purpose in your life. The word will not be fruitless; it will produce meaningful and beautiful results in your life. Raindrops do not return to heaven as raindrops; they must discharge their purpose on earth. In the same way, the word of God concerning your life will locate you. It will not miss your address because it is 'custom-made' for you.

> *"For as the rain and snow come down from heaven, And do not return there without watering the earth, Making it bear and sprout, and providing seed to the sower and bread to the eater, so will My word be which goes out of My mouth; It will not return to Me void (useless, without result), Without accomplishing what I desire, And without succeeding in the matter for which I sent it" (Isaiah 55:10-11)*

2. Christ's words carry the life of Christ. Jesus is the Word. "In the beginning [before all time] was the Word (Christ), and the Word was with God, and the Word was God Himself" (John 1:1). Jesus' words are not mere words, they have eternal life. Simon Peter was aware of this when he said in John 6:68, "Lord to whom shall we go? You have the words of eternal life."

The words of Christ can give life to a dead person, as well as nourish and maintain the life forever (Romans 8:11). This is why the scripture emphasizes that "Man shall not live by bread alone, but by every word that proceedeth out of the mouth of God" (Matthew 4:4, KJV). Christ's words nourish and minister life to every area of the recipient's life.

3. The word of Christ is the 'breath of God'. As one breath from God gave Adam's lifeless body 930 years of life (Genesis 5:5), so also does the word of God have the power to give life to every good thing that is dead or dormant in your life.

ATTITUDE TO CHRIST'S WORDS

Knowing the inherent power and possibilities of Christ's words should evoke an attitude of reverence in us. His words must be taken seriously and reverentially.

My children have the habit of saying, "Daddy said…" or "Mummy said…" The reason is simply because they know that whatever daddy or mummy says must be received and taken seriously. How much more should we honor every one of God's words!

God's words are not your uncle's or best friend's words. They are not even the words of your best mentor or even your parents. Your most admired personality may give you promises that may later not be fulfilled. This may be due to unforeseen circumstances or even due to a deliberate change of mind. But God is not man. He has the capability to fulfill His words and He will not change His mind.

God is reminding you through this book that His promises for you are His words and bond to you. As surely as God lives (God cannot die), every word He has spoken over your life will come to pass.

You must however believe God and His promises for your life. Whatever God has promised, do not allow Satan or any negative circumstance cause you to doubt God. His promises are forever settled, standing firm and unchangeable (Psalm 119:89). All of God's promises are forever 'YES' and 'AMEN' and you can be assured that 'YES' is the answer to everything and anything you can believe Him to give you. "For no matter how many promises God has made, they are "Yes" in Christ. And so through him the "Amen" is spoken by us to the glory of God." (2 Corinthians 1: 20).

"THE HOLY ONE…"

The holiness of God is the moral attribute, character and nature of God. God is spotless and sinless in His thoughts, actions and reactions. Everything that emanates from God is pure and good. By this, reader, God wants you to know that He forever wishes you well. His thoughts for you continually are thoughts of peace, not of evil (Jeremiah 29:11). Regardless of the lies of Satan and his agents, God cannot do you evil. He is Holy; there is nothing negative in Him or from Him.

In making reference to His holiness, Christ is saying in essence: "I am putting my character, my holiness, on the line concerning you. Whatever I say to you is said in my holiness." How refreshing and assuring!

In buttressing the above point, the Holy Spirit dropped this analogy into my spirit: Supposing a drunk promises to fix your pipe or a liar promises to mow your lawn. It will be correct to say of the drunk, that he promised in his state of drunkenness, and of the liar that he promised in his falsehood. None of the two can be trusted to keep to his words. This is the same concept being applied here. God makes promises in His holiness. Therefore, everything God has said and will say to you will be accomplished in His holiness.

David understood the power and dependability of

the holiness of God when he said, "God hath spoken in his holiness; I will rejoice, I will divide Shechem, and mete out the valley of Succoth." (Psalm 108:7).

David here wrote concerning the promise of God to establish him as a king. And while he went through many battles of life before the fulfillment of the promise, he was confident that the promise God had made in His holiness must come to fulfillment. He knew that no matter the battles that confronted him, his dynasty must be established. Consequently, he began to plan and declare what he would do with the things God had promised him.

Isn't this remarkable? David was yet to win all of his battles, yet because he fully trusted in the holiness of God, he started planning on what he would do after the promises were realized. He said in Psalm 108:7-9:

- I will rejoice
- I will distribute Canaan among my people
- Gilead is mine
- Manasseh is mine
- Ephraim is my stronghold and defense of my head

- Judah is my scepter
- Moab is my washbasin
- Edom is my slave, I will cast out my shoes over him
- I will shout victory shout over Philistia

LEARNING FROM DAVID

The above passage shows David praying and praising God at the same time. He also positively confessed that he would get the support of Ephraim and Judah. He saw, with the eyes of faith, all his enemies bowing and becoming his subjects. And then, in verse 13, he reiterated that his expected victory would come from God, by reason of His holiness.

Beloved, the God who promised you 'open door' has sworn in His Holiness. He will surely perform all things pertaining to you. You should, by faith, begin to thank God in your prayers for the things that are coming your way, just as David did.

Lord, I thank you for this reader. Doors of favor are open. Doors of promotion, enlargement and advancement are open. As Joseph received solution to the king's dreams, divine insight is released upon this reader for Holy Spirit-inspired ideas and solutions in Jesus name.

CHAPTER 5

THE TRUE GOD

As mentioned in the previous chapter, every title that Jesus used in introducing Himself is still very significant to you as a believer. We have looked at Christ's description of Himself as the "Holy One". Now we proceed to comprehend His nature as the "True One".

The Web dictionary defines truth as, "conformity with fact or reality." Truth also implies absence of lies, deception or shadiness. It is absoluteness of facts.

Christ, in describing Himself as the "true one",

wants us to know that there is no variableness or shadow of turning in God. He cannot lie. Satan is the liar and the father of liars (John 8: 44). Satan will use people or negative circumstances surrounding you to shoot deceptive thoughts of defeat into your mind. But you can always silence him and quench his fiery darts by holding firmly to God's promises concerning your life.

ATTESTED REALITY

Jesus can never lie. He can create or re-create whatever He wants to. People lie sometimes when they find it difficult to fulfill whatever promises they have made. But God is not people. He is not a vacillator. He is God. He is a promise keeper and performer.

> *"God is not like people, who lie; He is not a human who changes his mind. Whatever he promises, he does; He speaks, and it is done. (Numbers 23:19, GNT).*

When Jesus gives His word, every word is truth. You know why? Because when He speaks, He does not only give you truth, He is the TRUTH (John 14:6). I pray that the Holy Spirit helps you to see the synonymy of these words: Jesus, God, the Word, the

Truth, and the Spirit of Truth. Jesus is the Word, His Word is Himself, His word is true and also the Truth. Look at these scriptures again:

> *"In the beginning was the Word (Christ), and the Word was with God, and the Word was God Himself" (John 1:1).*

> *"Jesus said to him, "I am the [only] Way [to God] and the [real] Truth and the [real] Life; no one comes to the Father but through Me" (John 14:6).*

> *"Sanctify them in the truth Your word is truth" (John 17:17).*

> *"I will give you another Comforter... The SPIRIT OF TRUTH" (John 14:16-17).*

ASSURING REVELATION

What do these scriptures reveal? God is His word, His word is true, His Spirit (the Holy Spirit) is the Spirit of Truth. If God is the word, and His word is true, and God is the Truth, it means that everything about God is TRUE. This is what Jesus means by describing Himself as 'the True One'. Everything about Him is true. There is nothing deceitful in

Him, nothing two-faced, nothing fickle. (James 1: 17, MSG).

You can count on the unchangeableness of all the promises of God concerning your life. Things may look gloomy, situations may look impossible, but your God cannot lie to you. He is saying to you to count on Him because He is TRUE. You can count on His word. His word is the truth, not any negative situation or alarming report. Sooner or later, the truth will prevail over the negative condition.

Truth is the final report and final answer. Hold on to this truth: Whatever word that "THE WORD" (JESUS) has spoken over your life is the TRUTH. And it must surely produce positive results. Your God is the absolute; He is absolutely true, absolutely truthful and absolutely dependable!

THE KEY OF DAVID

Jesus further introduced Himself to the Philadelphian church as "He who has the key of David". There are two things we must quickly note here. First, Jesus says He holds THE KEY not a key, which means there is only one of such key, no duplicate. More importantly, a key signifies power, authority and control - and a key can lock and unlock doors!

The second point to note here is that Christ says HE is the one with the key of David. Several significant things in the Bible are tied to the name of David. These include: throne of David, house of David, seed of David, dynasty of David, tabernacle of David, and the key of David. Each of the above is significant, but what is the key of David?

The key of David is not like any other key, regardless of who owns the key or where it opens. The key of David is unique. The best definition I have for it is the one the Holy Spirit Himself gave me as I kept asking Him about the subject. The Holy Spirit impressed on my mind that the key of David is "the key of the continuity of David's dynasty to save and involve all nations." It is the master key that is all-encompassing in power and purpose.

SCRIPTURE POINTERS

In Isaiah 22, we read of Shebnah, who was the chief operations manager during king Hezekiah's reign. Shebnah had power and authority which he misused. God consequently removed him, even though he had considered himself irreplaceable (verse 25). He was replaced by Eliakim. I pray in Jesus name that whatever God has called you to do, you will be the one to do it. You will not be replaced by anyone; grace is released upon you to do exceedingly and abundantly above what is written of you.

Here is what God said of Shebna in Isaiah 22:20-24:

> *"On that Day I'll replace Shebna. I will call my servant Eliakim son of Hilkiah. I'll dress him in your robe. I'll put your belt on him. I'll give him your authority. He'll be a father-leader to Jerusalem and the government of Judah. I'll give him the key of the Davidic heritage. He'll have the run of the place—open any door and keep it open, lock any door and keep it locked. I'll pound him like a nail into a solid wall. He'll secure the Davidic tradition. Everything will hang on him—not only the fate of Davidic descendants but also the detailed daily operations of the house, including cups and cutlery." (MSG)*

Eliakim was given the key of David, the key of authority to rule and care for David's descendants.

Everything hung on Eliakim - the fate of the people, their well-being and their lives in general. Eliakim was a type of Christ. Moreover, his government was a type of Jesus' government. As Eliakim had the power to open and shut the door for the people, so Jesus said of the door in Revelation 3:7.

In Isaiah 9:6-7, the Bible says of Jesus and His dominion:

"For to us a Child shall be born, to us a Son shall be given; And the government shall be upon His shoulder, And His name shall be called Wonderful Counselor, Mighty God, Everlasting Father, Prince of Peace. There shall be no end to the increase of His government and of peace, [He shall rule] on the throne of David and over his kingdom, To establish it and to uphold it with justice and righteousness From that time forward and forevermore. The zeal of the LORD of hosts will accomplish this." (AMP).

So, the key of David, in reference to Jesus Christ, is revealed thus:

- Jesus fulfilled the Davidic covenant of 'throne of David' (Luke 1:32).

- Jesus has absolute power, authority and dominion (government is upon His shoulders). (Matthew 28:18).
- His kingdom is endless; He gave the church power to spread the good news to include the whole world.
- Jesus has the power to open or close the door of heaven.
- Jesus is the only way (the key) to God or access to the presence of God (John 14:6).
- Jesus is the door opened for believers into God's presence
- Jesus is the door closed against unbelievers from God's presence
- He has opened the door of heaven to those who will serve Him.
- He has closed the door of hell to those who will obey Him.

REFERENCE TO BELIEVERS

Those who believe in Christ are the most privileged and powerful people on earth. One reason is because Jesus has delegated the authority and power given

Him to His followers. In Revelation 3: 7, Jesus said:

"And to the angel (divine messenger) of the church in Philadelphia write: "These are the words of the Holy One, the True One, He who has the key [to the house] of David, He who opens and no one will [be able to] shut, and He who shuts and no one opens."

Every believer must know that Jesus has given immeasurable power and unlimited assets to them. He has given us:

- Key of power and authority.
- Key of access to God.
- Key to the heart of God.
- Key of praise.
- Key of good news, the gospel - to be spread all over the world.
- Key of opportunities.
- Key of utterance and unction.
- Key of wisdom.
- The master key that can open or close any door as a believer desires.

Dear reader, I pray that the Holy Spirit gives you understanding of the enormity of the power and authority that you have. One of my favorite scriptures in the Bible is John 14:14:

"If you ask Me ANYTHING in My name [as My representative], I will do it." (AMP)

I emphasized anything to let you know that, as a child of God, you are not supposed to worry, fret, or agonize over anything. Just ask the Lord in faith, believe and expect that what you have asked will be delivered very soon. Enjoy THE key, the master key of ANYTHING in His name!

CHAPTER 6

THE GOD THAT OPENS AND CLOSES

The last two introductory titles by which Jesus introduced Himself in our passage of consideration are opposite sides of the same coin. So, the explanations will have to be interwoven. Jesus introduced Himself as, "He who opens and no one will [be able to] shut, and He who shuts and no one opens".

This is awesome, to say the least. By this declaration, Jesus calls our attention to His omnipotence and sovereignty. He says He possesses unlimited power to do what He pleases, when, where, and how

He pleases, without offering any explanation. He is unquestionable. He is unstoppable. And, most importantly, when He speaks, or acts, no other power can change or reverse His decision.

BELIEVERS' COMFORT

God cannot be subjected to any earthly or spiritual court or jury system. He, however, can interfere and change the verdicts made by men. Lamentations 3:37 affirms His majesty:

> *"Who is there who speaks and it comes to pass, Unless the Lord has authorized and commanded it?"*

This means that the highest authority in your life or even in the world can never achieve anything in your life unless God allows or permits it. Wow, I love this! Negative plans and comments may be made and said about you, but they can never materialize except God allows it. This was one of the reasons Jesus told Pilate, "You would have no authority over Me at all if it had not been given to you from above."

This should gladden your heart as a follower of Christ. It is the God that you serve that has the final say over you. God however does not use His power anyhow. He acts based upon His overall wonderful counsel and plans. As we have established already, God is a holy God, and everything He does is predicated upon His Holy nature. This includes His use of power, which is dependent on His compassionate will. He does not use His power wickedly, because there is no wickedness in Him. He is a righteous judge.

So as a believer in Christ, knowing that God has the absolute power to do anything should build your faith. God is the most high God, higher than anything or anyone that may be making your life miserable. God is the God of possibilities, and there is nothing too difficult for Him.

PROOFS OF SOVEREIGNTY

A Christian couple had to undergo operation to remove one kidney from the wife to replace her husband's defective kidney. However, on the operation table, the doctors made an amazing discovery. They found three kidneys in the wife, instead of two! It turned out that the wife did not have to lose any kidney. God had demonstrated His power in their lives!

Let me show you another proof of the sovereignty of God. There was a king who became so successful. He became boastful of his success without any attempt to acknowledge or appreciate God. The king thought he was the 'all in all'. One day, however, he had a dream in which he saw himself as a great king who was suddenly removed temporarily from office.

The dream that this king had eventually manifested a year after. God humbled him because he failed to yield to God. As he was ruminating arrogantly over his achievements, the hand of God cut him down. He was sent into the wild for seven years to live with animals. The hair on his body grew like eagles' feathers and his nails grew like birds' claws. The king fell from grace to grass.

After seven years of living among animals, he had learnt his lesson. He demonstrated this by humbling himself before the Sovereign God. Here is his attestation of the sovereignty of God:

"At the end of the seven years, I, Nebuchadnezzar, looked to heaven. I was given my mind back and I blessed the High God, thanking and glorifying God, who lives forever: "His sovereign rule lasts and lasts, his kingdom never declines and falls. Life on this earth doesn't add up to much, but God's heavenly army keeps everything going.

No one can interrupt his work, no one can call his rule into question. At the same time that I was given back my mind, I was also given back my majesty and splendor, making my kingdom shine. All the leaders and important people came looking for me. I was reestablished as king in my kingdom and became greater than ever. And that's why I'm singing—I, Nebuchadnezzar—singing and praising the King of Heaven: "Everything he does is right, and he does it the right way. He knows how to turn a proud person into a humble man or woman." (Daniel 4:34 -37)

Dear reader, there is nobody in any position or status that was not helped or graced by God, including those who are not believers. Every good thing is from God to all mankind.

God had to show Nebuchadnezzar that although he was a high king, God was and still is the Most High God. I pray that anyone harassing you will be humbled by the Most High God.

In case you have been stuck on the same spot and your next level has been difficult and elusive, expect the anointing of God that worked for me during the writing of this book to come on you in Jesus name. And in case you are being tormented by people in higher authority than you, don't worry. God will show up to protect, provide, and demonstrate His power on your behalf in Jesus name.

If your own need is divine provision in any area of life, the Most High God will open His heavens and grant your heart desires in Jesus name.

> *"Say to them that are of a fearful heart, Be strong, fear not: behold, your God will come with vengeance, even God with a recompence; he will come and save you." (Isaiah 35:4, KJV)*

CHAPTER 7

INFINITE POSSIBILITIES

Did you observe something striking in the last introductory title of Jesus that we considered in the previous chapter? Let me show you, in case you missed it. Jesus described Himself as "He who opens and no one will [be able to] shut, and He who shuts and no one opens".

Did you notice that while Jesus says He has the master key (in chapter five) and that He has the sovereign power to open and to shut, He NEVER mentioned a DOOR? I asked the Holy Spirit for an explanation on this and here is what He impressed in my mind: Jesus has the key in His hand, and it is believed that anybody who has a key must be opening a door; but a door is not mentioned in the text because Jesus does not want us to limit the opening and shutting to physical doors only.

Jesus indeed has opened doors for us, but not just in the literal sense of the word door. Jesus has given us 'an open check' to whatever door we need open. Apostle Paul says in 1 Corinthians 16:9:

> *"For a great door and effectual is opened unto me, and there are many adversaries." (KJV)*

> *"Because a wide door for effective service has opened to me [in Ephesus, a very promising opportunity], and there are many adversaries". (AMP)*

> *"There is a real opportunity here for great and worthwhile work, even though there are many opponents." (GNT).*

> *"Because there is a wonderful opportunity for me to do some work here. But there are also many people who are against me." (CEV)*

You see, I purposely presented the different but complementary versions to show that doors are not just limited to physical doors. The Bible likens the door of preaching that opened for Apostle Paul as 'a wonderful opportunity'. Indeed, doors are wonderful and promising opportunities that are designed to beautify and decorate your destiny. The grand purpose is to empower you to do what you ought to be doing and to become who you have been packaged to become.

Open doors alleviate and even remove struggling, toiling, and frustration from a life. They remove every sense of worthlessness and uselessness from a destiny. May God open doors for you in high places and in all places in Jesus name.

DOOR OPENERS

God can use different people and different means to open doors for His children. If a person helps you to get into an area that can better your life, the person has opened a door of opportunity for you in that area. If you locked your key in your car, and a family member travelled to give you the spare key to open it, a physical door has been opened for you in that sense.

When King David offered Mephibosheth a better life to eat at the king's table for the rest of his life, a door of opportunity was opened for Mephibosheth (2 Samuel 9). When God caused a supernatural earthquake and doors of prison were opened for Paul and Silas, God opened literal doors for all the prisoners.

By the way, ordinarily, a physical earthquake would have destroyed the entire jail house, the jailors, the prisoners jailed, and everything in sight. It is only God that can cause a 'great earthquake' that will destroy only the things hindering His children. I pray that whatever divine shaking or earthquake that needs to happen will happen to release you into your purpose in Jesus name.

UNLIMITED ACCESS

The door that God has opened for you, dear reader, is an unending access to unquantifiable assets. You are receiving the master key that will lock or unlock doors as you desire. Expect doors to open in many ways for you, including:

- Door of opportunities
- Door of wisdom
- Door of favor
- Door of connections to helpers of destiny
- Door of connections to 'sent helpers'
- Door of monetary or financial resource
- Door of anointing
- Door of admission to schools or careers
- Door to businesses
- Door to knowledge or ideas
- Door of supernatural skills or divine endowment
- Door of eloquence or utterance

If you are a pastor, believe that God has opened your door to a successful ministry. If you are a student, you have been given the mind of creativity and the spirit of excellence. As a professional, it is time to step into the open door of insight, creativity and divine connections.

Indeed, the list of types of doors that God has opened for you is as vast as the vastness of God! God has granted you UNLIMITED ACCESS - step into your open doors in any area you so desire.

I have prayed that everyone that reads and recommends this book will experience unusual and supernatural doors opening up in great places. What you have not been able to achieve in years, you will achieve easily for reading this book and obeying God's instructions.

THE OTHER SIDE [OF THE COIN]

The last introductory description Jesus gave of Himself, according to our text, is: "He who shuts and no one opens".

As I have mentioned earlier, based on God's sovereignty, He has both the ability and the prerogative to open and to close doors. And this expression of sovereignty does not exclude His dear children.

You may ask, "Are you actually saying that God can close doors on His children?" Yes, this exactly is the idea here. There are events in life, such as business opportunities, admission to a college, marrying a lover or travelling to a beautiful resort that may look good to a Christian, but God can close doors of such opportunities. This is because God, who sees and knows the future, may already know that these things will be detrimental to the individual involved.

A lady, who had been single all her life, may suddenly find herself dating a man and everything seems to be going well, except that the man does not want to take the relationship to the next level. It may be God working to prevent the lady from a major disaster in the future. It may also be the devil closing the door of the lady's opportunity. The work of Satan in the opening and closing of doors will be dealt with in the last chapter. The point here however is that just because something, someplace, or someone looks good does not mean that God cannot close such doors.

In Acts 16:6-8, we are told that Paul and his group wanted to preach in Asia. Naturally, this would appear normal and commendable since they were going to preach the good news. Surprisingly, however, the Holy Spirit closed this door of preaching on Paul and his group. Isn't it interesting that the Holy Spirit did not allow Paul to preach?!

"Paul and his friends went through Phrygia and Galatia, but the Holy Spirit would not let

them preach in Asia. After they arrived in Mysia, they tried to go into Bithynia, but the Spirit of Jesus would not let them" [CEV].

Did you see that? The same God, who instructed the believers to go into the whole world and preach the gospel, disallowed Paul from doing His work in certain places. Yes, God closed the door on Paul. But as I said before, just because something looks good and promising does not automatically mean that it is God's will for us.

UNFAILING GOODNESS

What you must know, however, is that whether God closes or opens a door, He will never hurt you. Because He loves you unconditionally and cares for you deeply, whatever He does is always in your best interest. Even when things seem not to be going well for you, know that He is working behind the scene and He has the power to turn bad situations into good experiences for His children.

"And we know [with great confidence] that God [who is deeply concerned about us] causes all things to work together [as a plan] for good for those who

love God, to those who are called according to His plan and purpose" (Romans 8:28)

Are you a child of God? If the answer is a 'yes', then you have no cause to worry; trust in the Lord, give God time. Watch how He will wipe your tears, and cause you to laugh over what you have cried over. Sarah laughed at last after several years of crying due to barrenness; Joseph came out of prison despite hateful plots against him; Job rejoiced and received double blessing for his losses; Hezekiah was healed - somebody who was supposed to die within three days had fifteen extra years added to his life; Abigail had a better life after her first marriage; Peter was still used by God despite failing God; even the ungodly king Nebuchadnezzar was reestablished in his kingdom and was restored with better honor than what he had before.

Child of God, there is no door that has been closed on you that God cannot reopen with His powerful hands. There is no deal that seems lost that God cannot give you a better option. All you need do is walk daily with God, asking the Holy Spirit to help you. Be patient; no matter how long it takes for your answer to come, it will surely come and not elude you. God indeed causes all things (even the negative ones) to work out in the long run for His children.

OUR TESTIMONY

Permit me to share a personal testimony just to buttress this point of how God can turn negative experiences to work great things for you. This testimony is purely for illustration purpose.

An unpleasant situation happened to Dr. Festus and me some years back. We were in a partnership with some friends of ours that were also genuine Christians. Prior to the occurrence of the negative experience, God had visited Dr. Festus and me while in a forty days fasting. In the visitation, God said He wanted to separate us for an assignment. God spoke of so many things He would do through us. Some of those things are already happening, to His own glory.

However, somehow, Satan attacked our relationship with these good friends of ours. We were forced out of an arrangement we were in together. It was a very devastating experience. I could not understand how God would allow the closing of the door of such good relationship and arrangement. Due to the occurrence, many lies and damaging news were spread around about my family. I felt so disappointed, cheated, and humiliated. It was a very depressing experience, especially for me, because I was just a few years old in the Lord.

Things got so bad that it became shameful and unbearable for me to go to work daily. This was because the lies flying around were totally opposite to who my colleagues knew me to be. I became the talk of the office.

I wanted to tell our version of things, but God instructed us not to say a word. God actually used a ninety-year-old woman who I met for the first time in a nursing home to speak to me. I had gone on an errand to this nursing home to collect some things for a family member. One of the ladies I was sent to instructed me to wait in the lobby of the nursing home because she was still attending to a resident.

As soon as I sat in the lobby, there was an old lady who came out, walked carefully with her cane to where I was and sat right beside me. Instantly, she began to speak in tongues (gift of the Holy Spirit). I was perturbed but I knew God must have sent her to me. As this lady spoke in tongues, she also interpreted the message. To summarize the message, she said, "Be still, and you will know that I am God. If you want to be known, be quiet, the world will find you out".

Dear reader, that was an unforgettable supernatural occurrence in my life. My point is that, first, we did not want the door of the arrangement to close. Secondly, the seemingly right and obvious thing to do in order to clear our reputation was to defend ourselves. We realized however that it was God who had permitted the closing of this door.

A friend of mine actually told me that people were saying we were guilty, otherwise we would have spoken up. This friend of mine also wanted me to show our innocence, but God wanted us to be quiet. Not long after, God opened another door for us in the same place of failure. Men closed a good door against us, but because we obeyed God, He moved us to His divine plan for our lives.

SUCCOR IN CRISIS

Dear reader, does it seem like you are behind

and all doors are closed on you? Have you been lied against and robbed of your hard earned labor? Have you been used, rejected, and or frustrated? Do you feel you are in a pit and all hopes are gone? Cheer up. You serve a sovereign God, who is the creator of all things and all people. He has power over everything He has created, and He is willing and able to open any closed door.

God wants to restore what you have lost. He wants to give you what you have been longing for. From what I know of God through reading and experiential knowledge, He gives and restores superabundantly. This means superior in quality and excessive in quantity. God is never late, and there is nothing in heaven, on earth, or under the earth that is too difficult or too much for Him to give you. So, whoever has laughed at you, has laughed too soon. Whoever has shut good doors against you, is about to see the display of God's glory on you.

Let me reiterate the message of God through the old lady to you, "Be still and you will know that God is GOD." Calm down, and you will know that Jehovah is God (Psalm 46:10). God will make you to laugh last over every negative situation. Your laughter and rejoicing will be superabundant - much more than the tears you have shed - in Jesus name.

CHAPTER 8

GOD MAKES NO MISTAKES

I was on the treadmill one day (within the period of writing this book), when the Holy Spirit said to me: "Tell my people, I don't make mistakes." So, let me reiterate a point I made earlier. Whether God closes or opens a door, even if it is something or someone you want 'really badly', just obey God. Don't try to force God's door to the opposite direction - that is, if God opens but you want the door closed, please don't push to close the door; and if God closes a door, no matter what the situation is about, don't kick it open. Don't try to open the door God closes, and don't close the door He opens.

I have personally cried in great distress over the outcomes of some events in my life. There are times you're tempted to ask God: 'I thought you were the one that opened that door, why am I being abused? Why did I fail? Why did you not warn me before I got into this mess? I thought you spoke to me to do this, why do I feel so miserable?'

Actually, there are times as believers that we engage and enter doors that God has not opened. There are also times that we linger at doors that God has closed. And worst of all, there are times believers find themselves in doors opened to them by Satan. Yes, Satan can also open doors. But as I said previously, this will be dealt with in the last chapter.

DISCERNING GOD'S VOICE

For now, let us deal with this question. If God does not make mistakes, how does one know if He is the one opening or closing a door? Or if Satan can open or close a door, how does one differentiate between God's doors and Satan's schemes?

The answer is simple: Learn to properly recognize and discern God's voice. I read in a book sometime ago that people who can quickly differentiate between real money and counterfeits have one secret – they have studied and known the 'real' or 'genuine' money over time. Get to know the 'real' very well and you will be able to separate the real from the counterfeits. In other words, get to know the voice of God properly and you will not fall for Satan's counterfeit alternatives.

Look at the following few examples of those who walked with the Lord in the Bible and were asked by God to do outrageous things. Some of these men could have simply taken the instructions given to them as satanically induced or generated. How were they able to know the voice of God despite the fact that the messages seemed to be contrary to the ways of God?

- God told Hosea to marry a prostitute! (Hosea 1: 2)
- Abraham was told to kill Isaac before God later provided a ram as a substitute (Genesis 22).
- The Holy Spirit told Paul NOT TO PREACH in Asia (Acts 16)

How did Jeremiah know it was God asking

him to do the outrageous things He was asked to do? How would a prophet, a holy man of God like Hosea, be told to marry a prostitute? This was totally contradictory to God's instructions about priests. This was the point Peter made when God spoke to him in a trance. Should Peter even have the audacity to respond the way He did to God, when it was through open trance and not some hidden means that God used in speaking to him?

I believe Peter responded the way he did because he could not fathom how God would ask him to do what God Himself already instructed them never to do. As far as Peter was concerned, it was 'KOSHERLY' impossible for God to request for such a thing! (emphasis totally my formulation). You can read this encounter in Acts 10:9-15.

The methods of hearing God's voice as discussed here are not exhaustive. But as a child of God, I admonish you to please make it a priority to study His word more. Talk to Him more through prayers. Grow daily spiritually and ask God that His voice or hearing from Him means a lot to you. God sees all things. If you truly want to be hearing specifically from Him, He will know and He will personally teach and guide you.

A JOLTING EXPERIENCE

I became very desperate to grow deeper in hearing from God, after a loved one of mine died mysteriously. You see, a week prior to the incident, God showed me through a very vivid dream. I jumped up from my sleep immediately and I told Dr. Festus that I had just had a horrible dream about the individual's demise. The two of us just mumbled a prayer and I never remembered the dream again, until one week later when this precious person mentioned my name in the ICU and said, "Please release me, let me go; now I can leave". This was someone who had enjoyed good health and was not sick prior to this evil occurrence.

My loved one had travelled to another town a week prior to her death, but a day before the trip, she confided in our mom that she did not feel like going. She felt a resistance in her heart. Unfortunately, she went on the trip and her absence has created a major void in my family.

Obviously, God had spoken to me through that DREAM and He did same to my loved one through the INNER WITNESS. We both missed it! As I said before, I became desperate to properly discern God's voice after the occurrence.

Please don't wait till you have a similar experience like mine. Make discerning of God's voice a priority. It saves lives, gives peace and victory, and provides help and succor to people around you.

I referred to the sad incident above to show you that God speaks to all His children, but many of us are not accustomed to His ways of speaking and to His voice. It is possible that as you read this story, you also have your own stories of regrets or even stories of success on how hearing from God has impacted your life. There are many Christians who have become rich because God opened doors for them through instructions they obeyed. There are also Christians who are stagnated due to their immaturity in discerning God's voice.

GOD'S COMMUNICATION CHANNELS

So, how does one know when God is opening or closing a door? Or how do we know God's open doors and closed doors? I always teach that after everyone's born-again experience, the next most crucial thing is to learn how to discern the voice of

God. Here are few of the vehicles by which God speaks to people:

1. Through His Word (the Bible). The Bible is God talking to you. Pray before studying it, ask the Holy Spirit to give you understanding as you read it. Get the version of the Bible you can read and understand. All the other ways that God speaks to you must be subjected to the word of God. It is the final authority.

2. Through Dreams: Dreams are transactions or occurrences a person sees or is involved in during a state of slumber or sleep. Many examples in the Bible such as king Nebuchadnezzar in Daniel 4 and Joseph in Genesis 37 clearly demonstrate this.

3. Through Trance: Biblical scholars have identified trance as a sense of being taken or moved out of one's self or one's normal state. Let me simply define it as a supernatural revelation of divine message in which the recipient is suspended out of the body. I have been privileged to be in a trance once. I was definitely not asleep. I just felt a very nice feeling of divine presence in which I was kind of suspended in thin air. It was during this experience that I heard the audible voice of God for the first time. People who had similar experiences in the Bible include Peter (Acts 10:9-11) and Paul (Acts 22:17-18).

4. Through Visions: God made it clear in Numbers 12:6 that there is a difference between vision and dreams. A vision is almost the same as a dream except that a vision is seen or received while not asleep. A vision can come in form of pictures, symbols that may come like quick flashes or they may linger. God shows me visions a lot, especially during my private worship and prayer times. Some people receive visions from God while involved in their regular daily activities. Examples of people who received visions in the Bible include Ezekiel (Ezekiel 1:1); Abraham (Genesis 46:2); and Zechariah (Luke 1: 22).

5. Through the Holy Spirit: God communicates with believers daily through the Holy Spirit. If you are going to learn how to enjoy your walk with God, or if you are going to be a successful Christian, you have to be familiar with the voice and promptings of the Holy Spirit. The Holy Spirit is God Himself. He is the Spirit of God, living inside of the spirit of a believer to reveal the mind of God daily and to help us on earth.

Jesus said that the Holy Spirit WILL SHOW US THINGS TO COME. He will lead us and guide us. He will show you what eyes have not seen, nor ears heard (Read Romans 8:14,16, 26-27; John 14:26). The Holy Spirit speaks to us through: (a) word of knowledge (supernatural knowledge of things that are happening or that are yet to happen without prior information). God does not want to keep us in the dark, so He shows us things that are happening or things to come. The dream I had about my loved one was 'a word of knowledge' that showed me what would happen; (b) word of wisdom (not natural or common wisdom) - this is divine knowledge of what to do about a matter. This shows you God's plan, will, or purpose about a situation. It is divine solution. The old lady I met at the nursing home was used to give me divine wisdom.

The two most important avenues that the Holy Spirit uses to talk to us daily are through the inner witness and through the inner voice. I love what my General Overseer said in one of his teachings. He said, "If you depend on hearing from God only through dreams, what would you do when you have to make cogent decisions during the day? Would you go to sleep during the day, regardless of where you are?" This sounds humorous, but it is very vital to learn how to depend on the Holy Spirit for your daily guidance.

I said the Holy Spirit speaks through inner witness. This will come like an impression to your mind; it will come like a confirmation or a 'knowing' that this is what you ought to do. He will act as a 'witness' in your mind. If you want to make a decision about a matter where you have two options, and you pick option A instead of B, the inner witness comes to approve of your option or to disapprove of it. If you have peace about your option, that is a confirmation to go ahead. If you have agitations or resistance, it is a sign of disapproval. My loved one, who didn't feel like travelling, received such resistance. The Bible says the Holy Spirit is our 'STANDBY' [John 14:16]. He is always with us and stands by us. A witness according to Web dictionary is a, 'bystander', who confirms a situation or an occurrence. The Holy Spirit acts as 'Inner Witness'; A witness, who is inside to confirm an occurrence. He does that by giving you inner peace to give you a 'YES', and a 'NO' is when you just don't feel 'right' about the situation.

The second avenue, which is the inner voice, is the voice of the Holy Spirit Himself talking. This is when most Christians say, "I heard a voice but don't know whether it was my voice or God's voice or Satan's voice".

You will know it is God's voice because it will not be forceful; there will be no agitation, resistance, unrest or any tightness - only peace. The voice will come in phrases and or in long or short sentences. It normally comes as an impression into your mind. The voice comes to instruct, directs, or assures a believer.

I experience the inner voice of the Holy Spirit daily, because I have cultivated a habit of asking Him for almost everything I do. Being somewhat a 'perfectionist', I sometimes fret and agitate over things, but the Holy Spirit always comes to calm me. I am conversant in hearing Him say, 'Don't worry, I will Help you', 'Go and rest', 'Be quiet', 'Go and pray', 'You were not nice to....' 'leave her for now, the enemy has lied to her about you', and so on. Sometimes, He tells me what to ask people or tell them, when they come to me for advice.

The more you obey this voice, the better you get at identifying Him, even in the midst of millions of people. Identifying His voice gets easier as you learn to depend on Him and trust Him.

And at times when it seems like you can't hear Him at all, you can do what the disciples did in Acts 15:28. They made their decision based on what "seemed good to the Holy Spirit". This means, you should go ahead to do what you want to do as long as it is not based on selfishness, wickedness, and it is not outside of God's will.

Other means through which God can communicate with you include: divine messengers like pastors and other Christians (You must definitely verify this with the word and ask for confirmation). For a thorough explanation of this subject, the best teacher and expositor, apart from the Holy Spirit, that I know is Dr. Festus Adeyeye. He has many teachings on the subject. You can always log on to www.alccwinnershouse.org to avail yourself of the messages.

INTIMACY BRINGS UNDERSTANDING

The above are some of the major ways God talks to us daily. As you acquaint yourself daily with the Holy Spirit, you will be able to identify the 'doors' in your life. Getting intimate with the Holy Spirit daily has transformed my life. It has made hearing from God a continuous dialogue in my spirit all day. I deliberately talk to the Holy Spirit in practically everything I do daily. He talks back to me and guides me as I involve Him. I do this because I want to please God daily and it is through being guided by His Spirit that will make this possible.

Dear reader, Let me use this medium to provoke you to a deeper walk with God. If you are not already at the level of dialoguing daily with the Holy Spirit, then start it. Seek Him more, thirst for Him more, be desperate for HIM. If you dialogue constantly with Him or maybe you are even at a higher level, it is God's desire that you crave for more of Him.

I urge you not to park the car of your spiritual life at the level of salvation and confession, or even at your current level. Get deeper with God; move to a daily hunger for Him that will translate into daily transformation of your person and character. There are so many voices in the world, but it is your creator's voice which you hear and obey daily that has the power and capacity to make you who and what you ought to be.

God does not want you to be kept in the dark, He does not want you to live a life of continuous mistakes, or a life of trial and error; you can be divinely guided daily.

I pray that the Holy Spirit will help you to fall in love with God like you have never done before. I pray that your mind is cleansed and purged from all impediments hindering you from hearing your father's voice, in Jesus name.

CHAPTER 9

KEEPING YOUR COOL IN HOT SITUATIONS

One of the most powerful and practical ways to experience God as the God who opens and closes doors is to learn to keep your cool, especially when Satan, through people, is tampering with your 'doors'. From Genesis to Revelation, to the current period we live in, God has continued to prove Himself as the one with the final verdict in situations of life.

God already forewarned true believers that there would be trials, difficulties, hard times and stressful situations in life (see John 16:33). There are even times that a child of God will experience unanswered prayers; times when the heavens seem quiet and you cannot hear about a subject matter. What should you do? At pressure points of life (and everyone goes through such points), what should a Christian do?

When you find yourself in such situations, God wants you to keep your cool. Live your life daily by not looking at the situations confronting you. I have been through many challenges of life, so I know it can be very difficult when confronted with difficulties. Child of God, the doors that seem currently shut against you now are not unique to you alone. There are people who have been where you are, there are others going through the same things, and there are still others going through worse conditions due to closed doors on their dreams/plans.

I know that God can use me to minister to anyone going through challenges. This is because I have gone through different difficulties of life and God was the Rock I stood upon, the Pillar that held me, the Hand that shielded me and lifted me. God made my forehead stronger than every challenge that came my way. I can write pages of negative experiences, but the point I really want you to get from this is that hard times are synonymous with 'closed doors', and doors that are closed by people can be opened by God.

DIMENSIONS OF CLOSED DOORS

There are many examples of closed doors in life.

- What do you do when different doors are slammed shut in your face?
- What do you do, when a spouse wants out of marriage?
- What do you do when the body is ravaged with sickness?
- What do you do when you have been single all your life and you desire to be married?
- What do you do when you are rejected, mocked, shamed and disgraced?
- What do you do when facing eviction?
- What do you do when your immigration status is uncertain?
- What do you do when your child is in danger or children are unproductive and have shattered your dreams and hopes?
- What do you do as a Christian couple who had waited for years to raise godly children

but whose hopes to be pregnant medically, is zero?

- What do you do when people lie against you and 'it seems' they have gotten away with it?
- What do you do when there are haters all around you and you have not done anything to warrant hatred?
- What do you do when your life has not gone the way you planned it?
- What do you do, when 'it seems' nothing is working in your life?

The lists of different challenging situations or closed door experiences of life are endless. No matter what is confronting you today or will ever confront you in the future, there are answers provided in the bible. One of the answers that I find very practical and helpful, regardless of the situation, is in 2 Corinthians 4:16-18:

Having the revelation of these scriptures will radicalize your life. I love the scriptures so much and I want you to see it in three different versions of the Bible. 2 Corinthians 4: 16-18:

"So we're not giving up. How could we! Even though on the outside it often looks like things are falling apart on us, on the inside, where God is making new life, not a day goes by without his unfolding grace. These hard times are small potatoes compared to the coming good times, the lavish celebration prepared for us. There's far more here than meets the eye. The things we see now are here today, gone tomorrow. But the things we can't see now will last forever" [MSG]

"For this reason we never become discouraged. Even though our physical being is gradually decaying, yet our spiritual being is renewed day after day. And this small and temporary trouble we suffer will bring us a tremendous and eternal glory, much greater than the trouble. For we fix our attention, not on things that are seen, but on things that are unseen. What can be seen lasts only for a time, but what cannot be seen lasts forever" [GNT]

"Therefore we do not become discouraged [spiritless, disappointed, or afraid]. Though our outer self is [progressively] wasting away, yet our inner self is being [progressively] renewed day by day. 1

For our momentary, light distress [this passing trouble] is producing for us an eternal weight of glory [a fullness] beyond all measure [surpassing all comparisons, a transcendent splendor and an endless blessedness]! So we look not at the things which are seen, but at the things which are unseen; for the things which are visible are temporal [just brief and fleeting], but the things which are invisible are everlasting and imperishable" [Amp]

CHRISTIAN COMPORTMENT

When doors are closed, keep your cool, walk by faith. The Bible says that the way to keep your cool is not to put to mind the reality of the closed door. You should instead look and meditate on things you cannot see that are in the spirit realm.

The Bible says through the last scripture that there are two ways of 'SEEING A CLOSED DOOR'. Number one is seeing or looking at the closed door through your natural eyes and number two is seeing and interpreting the closed door spiritually. When you look and interpret things through your natural eyes, this is 'walking by sight' and when you look through the eyes of your spirit, it is 'walking by faith'.

As a Christian, you must use both your natural and spiritual eyes. You cannot deny the reality of the closed door - 'Looking not at the things you can see'. This means that though the closed door (no green card, no husband, no money) can be seen with your natural eyes, do not pay attention to it by dedicating your time to crying, depression or discouragement. Also ascertain with the help of the Holy Spirit if the closed door is a God-ordained closing. If it is, then trust the judgment of God that He loves you and wants the best for you. Besides, He knows what He is doing, He is faithful. No matter how long it may take, God will still make good His promise concerning the matter. This was what Sarah did, in another favorite scripture of mine (Hebrews 11: 11):

"By faith even Sarah herself received the ability to conceive [a child], even [when she was long] past the normal age for it, because she considered Him who had given her the promise to be reliable and true [to His word]." [AMP]

This was a major door closed against Sarah; the door had been closed beyond what the doctors could open. She was already passed the age of child-bearing. But the Bible says that Sarah judged, considered, regarded, counted, and trusted that God was trustworthy and would not fail to deliver what He had promised. Dear reader, this is the attitude you must have about God. As you wait patiently, walking with Him, He will surely get whatever door you want to open for you.

SEEING THE INVISIBLE

The second way to look at a closed door, based on the scripture above, is to 'look at what you cannot see'. Ask yourself this pertinent question: What can you not see? You cannot see someone who promised never to leave you nor forsake you. You cannot see the spirit realm, you cannot see God, His faithfulness, His past unchanging records, and His promises for your life. Your focus should be on God and His promises, your thoughts should be on the positive final conclusion instead of the negative reality.

What you should do is to begin to claim these promises upon the problem. You begin to speak God's words, speak what you want, not what you can see with your physical eyes. This was what God did in Genesis 1. When all that was there was darkness, God called out light from the spirit realm. So you also must learn to act like God. Every door and everything you need is in 'glory', in the spirit realm. You keep calling things you need from the 'unseen' realm into the 'seen' realm.

Remember, once again, that whatever doors that are currently shut against you are not unique to you. There are people who have been where you are, there are others going through the same things, and there are still others going through worse conditions due to closed doors on their dreams/plans. So, while you are waiting for the doors to open, keep your cool, be in constant dialogue with the Holy Spirit, enjoy your God and enjoy your life.

CHAPTER 10

ADVERSARIES OF YOUR DOORS

Are there doors in your life that have been opened or closed by God and some people are tampering with currently? You should always be prepared and be on the look-out to protect the blessings God has given to you.

Abraham, the father of faith, had to chase off 'evil' birds from messing up his next level (Genesis 15:11). Apostle Paul had many oppositions and attackers; Satan even hindered and impeded him (1Thessalonias 2: 18). In 1 Corinthians 16:9 He said,

> *"Because a wide door for effective service has opened to me [in Ephesus, a very promising opportunity], and there are many adversaries."*

The truth of open or closed doors by God is the reality of Satan attempting to close the doors God has opened. Satan rises as an adversary, using people, things, environments and satanic gadgets to tamper with your doors. Remember, however, that no matter how many avenues Satan is using to frustrate you, **GOD CAN OPEN DOORS THAT CANNOT BE SHUT BY SATAN AND PEOPLE.**

TAMPERING ROUTES

There are three main avenues through which your doors may be tampered with. These sources can cause closing of the doors that God has opened or opening of the doors that God has closed. I know you may be wondering: "But I thought you said God is sovereign and there is absolutely nothing that He cannot do".

Yes, you are so correct. But God will not do anything about these three avenues because He has given you power and authority to be victorious over them. You must also bear in mind that the covenant relationship believers have with God is a partnership, with a twofold dimension. God has His own role in the relationship and we also have ours. God's part of the partnership is called 'the divine part', while ours is known as 'the human part'. So, God will not take over your part; He wants you to grow up and do what you have to do.

In my household, for instance, my children have divided all the house chores among themselves. It is not uncommon sometimes to have some chores undone - for example, having unwashed dishes in the kitchen sink. If I call any of them randomly to wash the dishes, I am accustomed to hearing, "That is not my chore; I have done my own chore of washing the bathroom, doing the dishes is for Phillip".

Of course, all my kids know that whoever is with me in the kitchen at that point in time would have to do the dishes as I would not want to be looking for Phillip. All I want is a clean kitchen; it does not matter who will get it done. My kids know they don't have a say in the matter, I can force them to do their siblings' chores when necessary.

God however does not parent us like the parenting of earthly parents. God is a gracious father, who wants us to make choices based upon the 'will' He gave us. God will not force you or me to do anything, like earthly parents sometimes do. God did not force Samson from marrying Delilah. He did not prevent Abraham from impregnating Hagar. He could have disallowed Judas from betraying Jesus, but He did not; nor did He stop Cain from killing Abel. God will rather warn, direct and admonish us about things, like He did with Cain.

Why did God not intervene in these situations? As I already mentioned, He is not a forceful parent. He expects us to act based upon the willpower He has given to all of us. We all make hundreds or thousands of decisions daily - decisions such as what to wear, where to go, what to eat, who to befriend, and so forth. God allows you to voluntarily make these decisions. He will never impose on you what to do. He may suggest to you what to do, but the ultimate decision is yours to make.

I wrote all that to explain that the three sources that can tamper with your doors are simply your 'chores' or responsibilities. The sources are:

(a) You (b) People (c) Satan.

HOW YOU CAN TAMPER WITH YOUR OWN DOORS

You can close doors opened to you from God through:

1. Sinful living. Nothing is more detrimental to open doors as sin. Satan himself knows that righteousness is the surest safeguard to open doors. This is why he does all he can to entice you to violate God's word so you can be shut out of His open doors for you. What closed the door of the Garden of Eden against Adam and Eve? What prevented Reuben from enjoying the rights and privileges of a firstborn son? Why did many Israelites die on their way to the Promised Land? How did Saul lose his kingship? What led to the closure of Michal's womb? These examples and many more reveal the effect of sinful living on open doors. As Jeremiah 5:25 says, "Your iniquities have turned away these things, and your sins have withholden good things from you" (KJV).

Now, I must point out that sinful living is not restricted to obvious sins such as lying, stealing, fornication or adultery; it also involves less obvious but equally limiting practices such as malice, unforgiveness and bitterness. Bitterness and unforgiveness can shut your doors; they can block your prayers from being answered (read Mark 11: 25-26 and Matthew 6:12]. God loves and cares for you. He does not want you to be praying without results. So, forgiveness is a command, not an option (Mark 11:25).

2. Ignorance due to spiritual immaturity. The strength of Satan is deception, he uses believers' ignorance to sway them away from their godly benefits. Ignorance about God and ignorance about their new identity in Christ. Satan will always try to mislead you by manipulating your mind. Part of his 'chores' or assignments is to shoot negative thoughts into your mind and to deceive you about God, about God's plans for you, and about yourself. However, his tricks will only work on you if you choose to be ignorant or forgetful of God's promises and assurances concerning you. The Bible admonishes us to develop ourselves spiritually, so that "we will no longer be like children, forever changing our minds about what we believe because someone has told us something different or has cleverly lied to us and made the lie sound like the truth" (Ephesians 4:14, TLB).

A most assured way of building up our spiritual

lives is fortifying ourselves with the resources of the armor that God has provided for us. Ephesians 6:11 says "Put on the full armor of God [for His precepts are like the splendid armor of a heavily-armed soldier], so that you may be able to [successfully] stand up against all the schemes and the strategies and the deceits of the devil." Failure to keep to this often results in closure of open doors.

3. Inability to discern God's voice or not knowing how to hear from God. A Christian who is either too busy to hear from God or too easily distracted by different voices will easily jeopardize his or her open doors. Many have missed out on great opportunities in life because of this. This was why Jesus told Martha who was bothered that her sister, Mary, was prioritizing hearing from Christ above other things: "Martha, Martha! You are worried and troubled over so many things, but just one is needed. Mary has chosen the right thing, and it will not be taken away from her." (Luke 10:41-42, GNT).

HOW PEOPLE CAN TAMPER WITH YOUR DOORS

Satan can use people to tamper with your doors

by:

- Using 'good and well meaning' people to ignorantly give you wrong advice.
- Using anybody to deliberately give you advice that will tamper with your doors.
- Sponsoring haters, friendly enemies, co-workers, neighbors, and even strangers to tamper with your doors. I will show you a clear example of this in the case of Isaac in the next chapter.
- Using those in the occult, such as magicians, sorcerers, witches, star gazers, observers of times, fortune tellers, horoscope users and mediums (those who have evil spirits living in them, just like we believers have the Holy Spirit in us).
- Using fetishes as gadgets to carry out his evil assignments. Natural objects such as incense, stone, walls, mirrors and any object with evil anointing can be used as satanic gadgets to tamper with your door if you are not vigilant.

HOW SATAN CAN DIRECTLY TAMPER WITH YOUR DOORS

I cannot over-emphasize the spiritual evil assignment that Satan has taken up to make sure that all your doors swing in the opposite directions of what God wants. The only job Satan has is a threefold assignment: to steal, kill, and destroy.

Satan has so many names, few of which are: thief, murderer, devil, the wicked one, the destroyer, adversary, accuser, and he is your enemy. As God's name is significant when He introduced Himself to the churches, so also each name of Satan is loaded with evil meanings. Do not give him a chance into your life.

Apart from the fact that Satan can use you against yourself, or use accursed objects or people against you, Satan also has hosts of demons working for him to attempt to tamper and manipulate your doors. Two main ways that Satan carries out his evil assignments are:

[a] **Spiritual warfare in the spirit realm:** manipulation in the spirit realm using his evil

workers to destroy God's plans in people's lives (Daniel 10:12-13, 20).

[b] Spiritual warfare in the mind: manipulation through projection of negative and evil thoughts into the minds of people (2 Corinthians 10: 4-5).

Ephesians 6:12 says:

"For we are not wrestling with flesh and blood [contending only with physical opponents], but against the despotisms, against the powers, against [the master spirits who are] the world rulers of this present darkness, against the spirit forces of wickedness in the heavenly (supernatural) sphere." [AMPC]

All the forces mentioned in the scripture above are Satan's evil servants working with and for him to tamper with your doors. They are in four main evil ranks: principalities, powers, rulers of the darkness of this world, and spiritual wickedness in high places. The topmost and most wicked of this evil hierarchal order is – spiritual wickedness in high places, followed by rulers of the darkness of this world, then powers, and finally is principalities. Believers have been given power and authority over all of these evil forces

[Luke 10: 19]. Jesus has done His part by giving us power over 'all' of the power of Satan.

Remember, dear reader, that God is committed to doing His own part of the opening and closing of doors according to His will for your life. You are the one to fix the three sources discussed above through the power you have and your submission to the Holy Spirit. God has given you power to be victorious over all the three sources. If you can learn how to be victorious over these three sources, you will enjoy the doors set before you by God.

Lord, I thank you for the power and authority you have released upon every believer. Thank you for the open doors. I pray in Jesus name that this dear reader will rise up and maximize all the doors you have opened. I also pray that wisdom is released to keep all the doors you have shut, to remain shut, in Jesus name.

CHAPTER 11

POWER TO MAXIMIZE YOUR DOORS

I believe that with all you've read and discovered so far, you have been divinely positioned for boundless breakthroughs. This is your season of open doors. Unlimited access is granted for your next level.

Now that the tables are set before you, how do you maximize your doors? You do this through:

- Faith in God and His promises.
- Praise and worship.
- Prayer.

- Power of the Holy Spirit.
- Networking.

FAITH IN GOD AND HIS PROMISES

Faith is the main instrument to enjoy a victorious life as a Christian. Faith is like the 'currency' you need to purchase anything you want, (including the maximizing of your doors) from heaven. Faith is so vital for everything you do as a child of God, as the following scriptures reveal:

- Romans 1:17b: "As it is written, The man who through faith is just and upright shall live and shall live by faith." (AMP).

- Hebrews 11:6: "But without faith it is impossible to please and be satisfactory to Him. For whoever would come near to God must [necessarily] believe that God exists and that He is the rewarder of those who earnestly and diligently seek Him [out]. (AMPC)

- 2 Corinthians 5:7: (For we walk by faith, not by sight:) (KJV).

- Mark 11:22: "And Jesus, replying, said to

them, Have faith in God [constantly]" (AMP)

So, what is faith? Faith is trusting God and having confidence in Him and His words. It is trusting the faithfulness and ability of God to bring His promises for your life to manifestation. It is following God blindly and believing Him totally and completely, even when situations of life seem difficult.

Faith is needed to obtain your open doors but beyond this, you can further maximize the doors through faith. Isaac used faith in overcoming his challenges and maximizing his opportunities. Let me show you a few instances:

1. In Genesis 26, there was famine in the land Isaac was residing in. This was like a 'closed door' in Isaac's career - economic recession in his town of residency. Isaac wanted to relocate to another town because of the closed door. God however informed him not to relocate and Isaac obeyed because he had faith in God. His obedience soon opened doors of success and affluence for him.

What are the doors currently shut against you? What has God said through His words about the issues? Stand on the promises of God like Isaac did - your closed doors will open soon.

2. Isaac further maximized his open door by putting his faith into action. In the same chapter of Genesis, verse 12 says, "Then Isaac sowed seed in that land and received in the same year a hundred times as much as he had planted, and the Lord favored him with blessings." [AMPC].

Isaac maximized the open door God gave him by not being idle. Isaac was a farmer; he put his farming skills to use and God blessed him. For you to maximize the doors God has opened for you, you need to engage in self-reflection. What are you talented in? What are your passions? What do you do easily without breaking yourself?

Once you have identified your areas of strengths (they are some of the open 'doors' given to you by God), you should step out in faith to engage your passion. Transfer your passion into money generating avenue. As God blessed and prospered Isaac, so will you experience abundance in your efforts. It will however take faith in God and His promises for this to happen.

3. He maximized his doors by staying focused

amidst opposition. It may interest you to know that the door God opened for Isaac came with challenges and oppositions which he overcame. This is a fact of life. Open doors in whichever area you desire are always almost accompanied by challenges and oppositions. This may come as a surprise to many believers who wrongly assume that a door opened by God should be 'problem-free'.

In the case of Isaac, the king and the inhabitants of the land made things difficult for him but he persevered. Several wells dug by him were filled back with sand! (Genesis 26:16-22). This was a continuous closing of doors against Isaac's efforts. How frustrating this must have been for him! He however maximized the opportunity given to him by God by not wasting his time quarrelling with his opponents.

To maximize your open doors when you are faced with challenges and frustrations, stick to the original plan and promise of God. Do not quarrel with anybody. As I noted in the previous chapter, Satan may bring people or try to use events to frustrate you in the places of opportunities that God has given to you. But you must remain immovable. Do not quit, do not be discouraged, if you don't quit, the opportunity will still yield dividends.

PRAISE AND WORSHIP

Praise is appreciating and thanking God for who He is and what He has done. Worship is your affectionate devotion in which your love is communicated to God through your soul. It is the expression of a loving and grateful heart based upon your revelation of who God is. Praise, worship, adoration and thanksgiving are often used interchangeably.

How can praise and worship be used in maximizing open doors? Praise and worship will position you for hearing from God. Acts 13:2 says, "While they were worshiping the Lord and fasting, the Holy Spirit said, Separate now for Me Barnabas and Saul for the work to which I have called them." When you cultivate the habit of spending time in praising God, you are setting up your life on a pedestal of success.

Just as the Holy Spirit gave the disciples instructions for running the ministry, as you praise and worship God, you will begin to receive instructions on how to maximize your doors. Many

Christians have enjoyed promotions, favors and financial breakthroughs due to divine instructions received from the Holy Spirit. Pray to be a praiser and a worshipper - someone who deliberately finds time daily to thank and appreciate God.

Thanking God will usher supernatural turning around of difficult situations in your life. It is easy and natural to thank God when things are working well and there is no adversity. But your open doors will be better maximized if you cultivate a culture of thanking God in every situation. The Bible says in 1 Thessalonians 5:18, "In everything, give thanks: for this is the will of God in Christ Jesus concerning you."

Of course, you don't thank God for bad things; the Bible says, you thank God in it. This is what God wants us to do. When you learn to do this, unusual notable miracles always happen. Examples of such miracles abound in the Scripture. When Jesus thanked God at the tomb of Lazarus, Lazarus resurrected from the dead (John 11:41). When Jesus had to feed over five thousand people with the lunch of a little boy, all he did was give thanks to God and the people were fed and there were left overs! (Matthew 15: 36). The leper who went back to thank Jesus for his healing, got a better deal than his colleagues (Luke 17:16). King Jehoshaphat was in a battle and he set praisers who were thanking God saying, "Give thanks to the Lord, for His mercy and loving -kindness endure forever" (2 Chronicles 20:21). What followed was that their enemies turned against each other.

So, cultivate the habit of thanking God daily. And because God does not change, supernatural miracles such as life coming upon a 'dead' marriage or business, abundance of provision, and enjoying peace all around will be your experiences.

PRAYER

Prayer is a mighty weapon that Jesus has given to His followers for unparalleled victorious living and maximization of God's provisions for them. Jesus showed that prayer was important because He Himself prayed often. He emphasized that prayer must be a daily and continuous exercise. He said 'WHEN' you pray, not 'IF' you pray (Matthew 6:5). Through prayers, you can harness and enjoy every benefit Jesus died to give believers.

Prayer is communication with God. It is a 'two-way" communication process, whereby a believer talks to God and God talks back to the believer. So prayer is also a way to hear divine instructions from God. And hearing divine instructions is a main ingredient for maximizing your open doors.

The roles of prayers in maximizing doors cannot be over-emphasized:

1. It helps to open doors closed by Satan and his cohorts. In Acts 12:4-10, Herod the king imprisoned Peter, with the intention to kill him. The church gathered and prayed for Peter. Due to this prayer, an angel of the Lord appeared in the prison and delivered Peter. Prayer can open literal doors closed by people. In the case of Peter, it was a literal door. In some countries, Bibles and Christian teachings are not permitted in the lands. However, through prayers, there are Bibles and sermons accessible to people all over the world through the Internet.

There was the case of a Christian sister who was frustrated by her direct supervisor who refused to promote her. Through prayers, however, God removed the wicked supervisor to another location and the sister was promoted. Doors of businesses, education, and opportunities have been opened to many people due to the power of prayer. Are there doors shut against you anywhere? Take the challenge to the Lord in prayers. He will grant your petitions.

2. Through prayers, opportunities lost in the past can be regained. Manoah, the father of Samson, was not with his wife, when the angel first appeared to her. He however prayed to the Lord (in Judges 13:8) to send the angel again to re-instruct him and his wife. God heard his prayers and the angel revisited them.

Samson also provided us with an example of effectiveness of prayer. He had failed to maximize his purpose among the Philistines. But when he prayed to God to revisit him one more time by restoring his strength so he could correct his errors, God granted his prayers (Judges 16:28). As a believer you can regain your lost grounds, missed opportunities, wasted open doors, and valuable relationships through prayers.

3. Through prayers, you can be divinely guided into your open doors and breakthroughs. In 1 Samuel

30:8, David prayed to the Lord and was instructed on the outcome of his pursuit. Believers should learn the habit of faithfully communicating with God in order to maximize doors of life.

4. Prayer can be used to maximize your doors in any area you desire. Jesus gave prayer as an 'open check' to obtain ANYTHING from God. In John 14:14, He Jesus said, "If you ask Me anything in My name [as My representative], I will do it."

Knowing the boundless possibilities you have through prayer, Satan will use every scheme and deception on you to stop you from praying. All he is targeting is to stop you from maximizing your open doors. Fight prayerlessness with every strength in you. Have a time selected and allotted exclusively daily for God. This will help transform your life in all areas.

Jesus says in Matthew 18: 18: " I assure you and most solemnly say to you, whatever you bind [forbid, declare to be improper and unlawful] on earth shall have [already] been bound in heaven, and whatever you loose [permit, declare lawful] on earth shall have [already] been loosed in heaven."

Take this verse seriously. You can transact businesses in heaven while on earth. You are not an ordinary person; you have the power of God. Whatever you bind or declare as improper on earth, is also bound and declared as improper in heaven. There may be ancient doors in your family that are improper, unlawful, and should be removed; remove them through prayers. Through prayers, open doors of favor with your employer, supervisors and mentors, will open up. Through prayers, you can receive resources of people and money. Through prayers, you can receive divine instructions that will lead to unstoppable promotions.

Take a few minutes right now, to put into practice what you have just read. Thank God for the love and mercy He has shown you. Thank God for the unseen battles He has won for you, the food you ate that you did not choke on, and His general protection and provision for your life.

POWER OF THE HOLY SPIRIT

The Holy Spirit is God living inside of every believer. Any believer that wants to live a victorious Christian life must learn to cultivate a daily intimacy with the Holy Spirit. The Holy Spirit is the believer's Comforter, Counselor, Helper, Advocate, Intercessor, Strengthener, and Standby. He can help you to maximize your open doors in the following ways:

1. The Holy Spirit can endow you with the talents, gifts and resources you need for new 'doors' and maximizing what you already have. In Exodus 31:2-5, God says, "See, I have called by name Bezalel son of Uri, the son of Hur, of the tribe of Judah. And I have filled him with the Spirit of God, in wisdom and ability, in understanding and intelligence, and in knowledge, and in all kinds of craftsmanship, To devise skillful works, to work in gold, and in silver, and in bronze, And in cutting of stones for setting, and in carving of wood, to work in all kinds of craftsmanship."

As these verses reveal, it was the Holy Spirit who equipped and empowered Moses' workers to be able to construct the Tabernacle. Learn to ask for specific resources that you need to make you outstanding and effective in your chosen field. Solomon asked for wisdom (2 Chronicles 1:10); Apostle Paul asked for utterance (Ephesians 6:19). A student can ask for excellent spirit; a care-giver can ask for a compassionate heart and healing hands. Indeed, the lists of things you can ask to be endowed with is endless, you have been granted open doors that cannot be shut.

2. The Holy Spirit is the believer's Guide. A guide is someone who assists in leading and directing a person to a desired destination. From the Old Testament to the New, the Holy Spirit has been actively involved in guiding, instructing and helping God's people. In Genesis 1:2, He moved over the earth to structuralize the earth; in Acts 8:29, He instructed Phillip to preach to the Ethiopian eunuch; in Acts 11:12, he instructed Peter to travel; in Luke 4:18, He anointed Jesus; in Matthew 4:1, He led and guided Jesus; in Acts 16 6-7, He prevented Paul and Silas from preaching in Asia and Bithynia.

Cultivate the habit of asking the Holy Spirit for everything before you do anything; the path of your life will shine better and better, from failure to success. This is because the Holy Spirit will give you wisdom and instruction for daily living and success.

3. The Holy Spirit will mold you to conform to the image of Christ. One of the benefits of this in relation to maximizing your open doors is that it

helps to develop in you, people skills. People skills help you get along well with others and can easily get you promoted in your career. Galatians 5:22-23 says: "But the fruit of the [Holy] Spirit [the work which His presence within accomplishes] is love, joy (gladness), peace, patience (an even temper, forbearance), kindness, goodness (benevolence), faithfulness, Gentleness (meekness, humility), self-control (self-restraint, continence). Against such things there is no law [that can bring a charge].

These are the character traits the Holy Spirit wants to give you in exchange for negative habitual traits. There was a man, a Christian, who kept losing his jobs. He would be gainfully employed and would be fired after a few months. The man kept saying he was not liked and was being persecuted because he was a Christian. It however turned out, after careful investigations, that this man was lazy, had bad work etiquette, and was not submissive to the authority of female supervisors.

Through the power of the Holy Spirit, people can be molded into 'newness' in Christ. However, any believer that wants a change of character must yield daily to the Holy Spirit, asking for His transforming power. When believers all over the world cultivate the habit of leaning upon the Holy Spirit for character transformation, there will be trends of success in families, businesses, and the body of Christ can maximize the open doors Jesus has given to us.

4. The Holy Spirit guides and teaches believers ALL truths (John 16:13 -15). Truths about God, about yourself, about other people, about the world, and about Satan will be communicated to you through the Holy Spirit. Truths known will empower you to be free from sins, addictions, negative people, the world, and Satan.

The Holy Spirit will also give you wisdom for your daily living and decisions of life. As you obey Him, you will always be at the right places, at right times, with the right people, doing the right things, and achieving the right results. He will deliver messages from God to you. He will show you and guide you into God's plans, purposes and will for your life. He will let you know which doors are open and closed. He will let you know if doors are from God or Satan. He will teach you what to do about doors and how to maximize your doors.

The Holy Spirit will announce, show you, and

declare the things that are to come. You will not be in the dark or be confused about what to do. The Holy Spirit will teach and show you the future. Many Christians have been spared untimely death, aches and agonies from toxic relationships, and loss of money from bad investment decisions due to the promptings of the Holy Spirit.

You can take a moment to talk to the Holy Spirit right now. Ask Him to anoint every area of your body, ask Him to pour great grace upon your destiny. Ask Him to be everything Jesus wants Him to be in your life. Pause a moment after this prayer, maybe, you may hear His promptings. Do this daily during your prayer time; you will start hearing the Holy Spirit, more and more.

NETWORKING

To maximize your open doors, you must learn not to be 'bound in a box'. Be flexible; make every effort to avail yourself of new insights and opportunities. Paul and Silas maximized their open doors. They 'moved from city to city', to preach the gospel. (Acts 16:11-13).

To maximize your open doors, be open-minded enough to 'move from people to people'. This means to educate yourself by networking with others, talking to different people, from different places to advance your career, marriage, business, and health. Whatever door God is opening or has opened for you, chances are that some people have successfully walked the path before. Connect with such people.

Interestingly opportunities abound in many ways today and take various forms. You don't even have to travel from city to city literally, like Paul and Silas. You can reach the whole world through the Internet and the social media from your bedroom!

Paul and Silas further maximized the door opened to them by connecting to a 'helper of destiny'. For instance, in Acts 16:14-15, they met a lady, Lydia, who became their 'landlady' immediately. The lady and her household became baptized through learning more about God from Paul. Lydia provided both accommodation or 'hotel' expense and food expense for Paul and Silas.

To maximize your open doors you need people, who will be financiers or sent helpers to foster your door. Do not be snobbish, obnoxious, arrogant, or unapproachable. Character traits such as these can shut doors of helpers.

Dear reader, Jesus has given every believer the power to overcome all challenges of life. He has opened for us doors of success into every profession and doors to peaceful and victorious family living and community unity. He has shut doors against failures, hardships, struggling, and toiling. He has given us power to be victorious people. You have the power over the evil one and all his cohorts. Arise, eat, the tables are set before you, open door is within your reach, limitless access are granted to you in Jesus name!

CONCLUSION

Let me conclude by asking you these vital questions:

IS YOUR DOOR OPEN OR CLOSE?
a] Yes
b] No
c] Yes/No
d] I don't know

e] All of the above

Other questions you should answer are:

WHICH DOORS ARE OPENED?

WHICH DOORS ARE CLOSED?

My last question for you is:

WHAT ARE YOU GOING TO DO ABOUT YOUR DOORS?

> Avail yourself with the prayer book:
> **PRAYER BUFFET FOR OPEN DOORS**

THE GREATEST PRAYER

The greatest prayer of a lifetime is to be reconnected back to God in a living relationship. Relationship is the basis for asking. You cannot pray to a God whom you don't know and who does not know you. God wants to be intimate with you. This type of relationship is available to each one of us when we sincerely repent of our sins, and ask God's forgiveness, and receive His Son, Jesus, as our personal Lord and Savior. If you have never surrendered your life to God, or if you have turned away from God and you want to return to Him, now is the time. God is waiting for you. His arms are open wide to receive you. Just pray this simple prayer right now:

O Lord, be merciful to me, a sinner. I realize that I am a sinner. I need a savior and you are my savior. I repent of every sin, every wrongdoing, and I ask for your forgiveness. I receive Jesus Christ, Your only begotten Son, as my Lord and my Savior. I believe that Jesus went to the cross for me and paid the price for my salvation, and now I receive Him into my heart. I declare that I am born again. I am a child of God. Old sins are gone, and I have a brand-new life in Christ in Jesus' name. Amen.

I WOULD LOVE TO HEAR FROM YOU!

Thank you for purchasing this book. I would love to hear from you, but even more than that, I would love to pray for you and write back to you. I hope you will let me know what you are believing God for, so we can join together in agreement and turn our faith loose for miracles. I look forward to your testimony!

Send your prayer requests to me at:

Dr. Anthonia Adeyeye
Adeyeye Evangelistic Ministries (AEM)
P.O Box 810
West Hempstead, NY 11552
E-mail: dranthonia@alcministries.com
Website: www.alccwinnershouse.org

www.ingramcontent.com/pod-product-compliance
Lightning Source LLC
LaVergne TN
LVHW051840080426
835512LV00018B/2994